100
ACTIVITIES
FOR SCHOOL KIDS

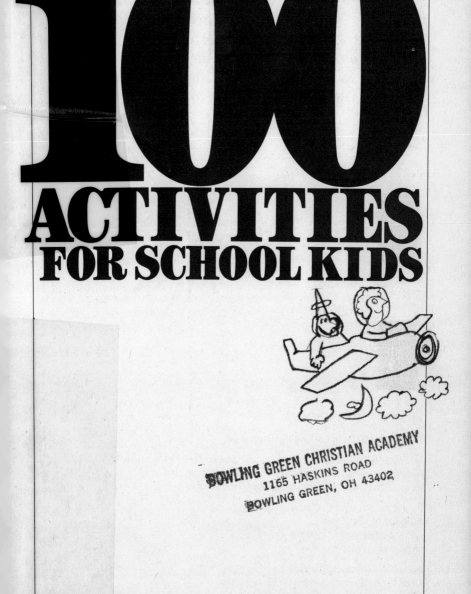

Here are 100 activities you can use in your classroom or at home with school-aged kids. Most of these activities are designed to be done by groups of children; some are designed for families to do together; and others are meant for kids to do on their own. All 100 ideas are intended to help kids have fun and learn about God and His love for them.

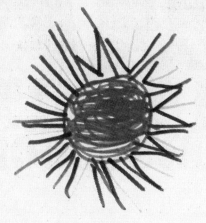

100 ACTIVITIES FOR SCHOOL KIDS

© 1989, 1998 David C. Cook Publishing Co.

Published by David C. Cook Publishing Co.
4050 Lee Vance View
Colorado Springs, CO 80918
www. cookministries.com

Edited by Dave and Neta Jackson
Design: Christopher Patchel and Dawn Lauck

Printed in the United States of America

ISBN: 1-55513-139-5

Contents

BIBLE GAMES

1 Commandment Charades

Copy each of the Ten Commandments from
Exodus 20:3-17 on a different strip of paper and
put into a container. Each person takes a turn
drawing a paper and acting out the commandment written on it. No words can be used, only
motions. Other players try to guess the commandment.

2 Helping Charades

Start by reading Matthew 25:35-40. Each player
thinks of one way to follow Jesus' example of
doing good deeds. Take turns acting out your
ideas without words. Other players call out what
they think the actor is doing. After the game,
each player should choose one idea and do it to
show Jesus' love.

3 Bible Scramble Boxes

Gather lots of empty tissue boxes and cover the sides with a light color of poster paint or construction paper. Put the boxes in a line and print part of a memory passage on each box. Put the Bible reference on the last box. Turn over all the boxes and print a second passage on a different side. Do this for up to six passages, using the six sides (and ends) of each box. Use a different color marker for each passage.

Now mix up the boxes. Roll the box with the references and see which reference is on top. Place the boxes so the sides facing up show that passage in the right order.

4 Mental Rebuses

Encourage kids to make up thought pictures to help them remember the words of a verse. *Example:* A heart and a book could be reminders of "I have hidden your word in my heart" (Psalm 119:11).

5 Puzzle Swap

Choose a familiar Bible story: the Resurrection (John 20:1-18); the Christmas story (Luke 2:1-18); or the Good Samaritan (Luke 10:30-37). Read the story together. Hand out blank sheets of paper. Each person creates some kind of puzzle about the story: a crossword, riddles, scrambled letters, rebus, word search. Then trade puzzles and have fun solving them.

6 Bible Charades

On separate slips of paper, list Bible references for familiar, action-filled Bible stories: I Samuel 17—David and Goliath; Exodus 14—crossing the Red Sea; Judges 16:26-30—Samson's death. (Choose others, but list only the Bible references.) Put the slips in a bowl and let each person draw one. After everyone's looked up his or her reference, take turns acting out the stories. Keep track of the time it takes the "audience" to guess each charade. The person whose story is guessed in the least amount of time wins.

7 Famous Family Game

Sit in a circle. One person starts by naming a member of a famous Bible family ("Adam"). The next person must name another member of that family ("Eve," "Cain," etc.). Go around the circle until the family is as complete as you can make it. Then start a new Bible family and repeat the process. Score one point for each family member added to the original name.

8 Bible Baseball

Divide players into teams. "Pitch" players on Team A questions about Bible heroes. If a player answers a question correctly, he or she gets a hit. If not, it's a strike. Three strikes and the team is out—and Team B is up. Four hits and the team scores a run or point. Keep going back and forth for a specified number of innings. The team with the most runs wins.

9 Who Am I?

Play a guessing game to remember Bible stories about people who chose God's side when there was a conflict. Each person picks a story and a character from the Bible. *It* gives one clue; then others guess *It's* story and character. For more clues, players can ask questions that can be answered with *yes* or *no*.

Stories to choose from might include: Elijah (I Kings 18); Paul as a prisoner (II Timothy 4:5-22); Paul shipwrecked (Acts 27: 1—28:16); Daniel and his friends (Daniel 1); Daniel's friends (Daniel 3); Daniel in the lions' den (Daniel 6).

10 Truth and Error

Play a Bible quiz game to see whether the players know the difference between Bible truths and errors. Choose some verses to read aloud from the Bible—for example: Ephesians 4:24; Romans 12:1; II Corinthians 5:20; I Timothy 1:15. Read some verses just as they are written. In some verses, change a word or add a "not" to make the meaning of the verse wrong. Let players vote on whether what you read is truth or error. Talk about why it is important to know and to follow what is true.

11 Who? What? Where?

How much do players know about the life of Paul? Everybody can help to make up questions about Paul, starting with the words WHO, WHAT, or WHERE. Examples: WHO spoke to Paul on the road to Damascus? WHAT happened when Paul and Barnabas argued about taking John Mark with them on a missionary journey? WHERE was Paul shipwrecked?

To play, form two teams. Search Acts 9 and chapters 13—28 for good questions. Write each question on a separate slip of paper, along with the answer, and sort them into categories of WHO, WHAT, or WHERE. A player on Team A picks a category—who, what, where—and is asked a question pulled from the pile of slips of paper in that category by Team B, then vice versa. The team with the most right answers wins.

12 Bible Book Scramble

Write the name of each book of the Bible on a separate 8 1/2" by 11" piece of paper. This can be done in advance, or assign kids various names of books to write. If they wish, they can decorate these "game cards" as they choose. After all 66 books have been completed, scramble the sheets of paper and see how long it takes the children to place them in the proper order. This game can be played as a group with the object being to get the books in the proper order more quickly each time. Or it can be played as teams to see which team is the fastest.

13 Bible Alphabet Game

Starting with the letter A, have children search through their Bibles to locate a person, place, or thing that begins with that letter of the alphabet. Have them write down the word and the Bible reference and then move on to letter B. See who can get to Z first. Letters Q, X, and Y will be tough, but they're in there. You may want to skip those letters depending on the age of your children. After a winner is declared, identify or talk about the meaning of unfamiliar words that the kids discovered.

CLASSROOM ACTIVITIES

14 Time Game

To play the Time Game, one person keeps time with a watch that has a second hand. Each player holds up his or her hand. When anyone thinks 120 seconds have passed, that person puts down his or her hand. The person closest to the right time wins. See how long two minutes seem!

Discuss what this game might tell you about God's view of a long time. Why does He sometimes seem to take a long time to answer prayers?

15 Shadow Fun

For each activity you will need a bare wall and a floor lamp with an extra-bright bulb. Demonstrate these ideas; then let your kids have a turn:

Hand Shadows. Hand shadows are fun and easy. Hold your hands between the light and the wall. Then move your fingers and hands to form shadows of animals, birds, or people. Tell a story to go along with the shadows your hands make on the wall.

Body Shadows. All you need is yourself. Stand between the light and the wall. Then bend, stretch, jump, and watch your shadow mimic your actions. Make up shadow motions to go with a favorite Bible memory verse. Try Isaiah 40:31 to start.

Shadow Puppets. You need cardboard, tape, and straight sticks. Cut out several shapes to tell a Bible story like Jonah and the whale. Tape a stick to the back of each shape. Hold your puppets between the light and the wall. Make the shadows of your puppets act out the Bible story.

16 Christian Stars

Do your kids have a favorite singer, football player, or actor who you know is a Christian? Start a collection of their pictures. Tell kids to look for interviews with these people in newspapers and magazines. How are they different from other stars?

Write out and put up verses that explain how Christians try to live. Start with these: Romans 2:6, 7; Galatians 6:9; Philippians 1:27; I Thessalonians 5:16-18.

17 Sundays Past

Find out what people used to do on Sunday many years ago. Assign kids to ask their grandparents and elderly neighbors or people in your own church these questions: What kind of church did you go to? How did you get there? What was your Sunday school like? What did you do Sunday afternoons? Encourage the kids to tape-record the answers for class.

18 What Is It Like?

Have kids pretend they are the man with the crippled hand—the one Jesus healed on the Sabbath day. Bring bandannas or strips of cloth to use as slings. Help kids tie their hand in a sling for the class period. Tell them to try to tie their shoes, write, and do other things using only their free hand. Afterwards, imagine how the crippled man must have felt after he was healed. Say a thank-You prayer to Jesus for your hands. Vary this activity according to the disability found in other Bible stories that you teach such as being blind, hearing impaired, or lame. Reinforce to children how much God loves and values every individual—including those with disabilities.

19 Prayer Partners

Have kids choose a classmate for a prayer partner. Partners should agree to pray for each other every day. They could exchange some sort of visual reminders of each other, such as a class picture, to keep at their bedsides. Then, at least once a week, they should share daily ups and downs with each other. Be sure to share God's answers to prayer, too. Change partners at the end of the month.

20 Prayer Chain

Set up a prayer chain among class members. Make copies of names and phone numbers and give one to each person in the chain. When someone needs a prayer, anyone on the list can start the chain by calling the number beneath their number on the list. The person at the bottom calls the one at the top, etc. Use the chain for thanking God for answered prayers, too!

21 Older Friends

Get a list of your church's senior citizens. Invite them to your class for a get-acquainted time with the kids. Mark each senior's birthday on a class calendar and make sure you remember it by sending a home-made card signed by the whole class.

22 Play-Back Bible Sounds

Turn on a cassette recorder for fun and inspiration.

• Dramatize and tape an exciting Bible story. Assign parts (don't forget a narrator) and add sound effects for an old-time "radio drama." (This will take some pre-taping rehearsals.).

• Ask different kids to read their favorite Bible verse or story and tell you what it means to them personally while you record their words on tape.

• Choose a favorite psalm to read and record as a class. Play soft music on a record or radio for a background as you read.

• Be an "on-the-scenes Bible reporter." Assign kids to take roles of Bible characters. Tape a straight reading of a Bible story. Then leave the tape running and interview "Bible characters" about their feelings and reactions to the event that just happened.

Make gifts of these Bible tapes by sharing them with shut-ins.

23 Welcome Wagon

As a Sunday school class, reach out to a new family in your community—perhaps one from another country. Make a list of helpful names and phone numbers: doctor, dentist, emergency numbers, schools. Make a welcome visit with some homemade goodies. Learn the name of each one in the new family. Invite them to your church and make sure each family member gets to the right Sunday school class. Have a welcome party or an outing with the new family and invite the families of your students to join you.

24 Persistent Prayer

People talk more about answered prayers than prayers they have been praying for a long time without getting an answer. Ask a missionary, a pastor, a Sunday school teacher, and a grandparent to share one prayer request they have had for at least a year. They might even be willing to share the prayer they have been praying the longest. Pick one or more of these prayers. Tell the person your class will join with him or her in praying for the special need. Encourage this person by sending him or her a postcard with a Bible reminder that God always hears and answers prayers. (Check Matthew 18:19, John 15:7, I John 3:22, and Psalm 91:15.)

25 To Tell the Truth

Have your kids test their truthfulness in a tight spot. Roleplay these problems:

• You are talking about someone and he walks in.

• You dropped your dad's camera. He discovers it doesn't work.

• You were watching TV and forgot to give your mom a message. She ended up missing an important meeting.

Have kids discuss different ways each situation could be handled. What are the strengths and weaknesses, if any, of each?

26-29 Time Capsules

How about making a time capsule that freezes time while it helps your class save information about your church today for the church of to-morrow? If you are going to bury your time cap-sule outside, you will need a metal, waterproof container. Or, pack everything in a sturdy card-board box, label it, "Not to be opened until _____" (the date you decide on). Seal it with masking tape and store it on a shelf.

Here are a few ideas for what to put in your time capsule. Choose one—or do them all!

26 Capsule I: Facts and Faces

Make a class photo file. Borrow a camera for snapshots, then glue these on index cards or sheets of paper. Allow everyone to fill the rest of the paper with information about themselves: height, favorite food, future occupation, favorite Bible story, etc. Make up a list of fun informa-tion; then be sure to have everyone sign the cards.

27 Capsule II: Monthly News

Collect all the news from your church for a month: newspaper clippings about church events, church bulletins, newsletters of different ministries, calendar, flyers announcing special activities, a church directory.

28 Capsule III: Future Wishes

Get some wishes for your church's future—
either on paper or on cassette tape. Encourage
everyone in your class to complete the sentence:
"One thing I really hope our church does within
the next five (ten, twenty) years is _____." If
you put the wishes on paper, have each person
sign the wish. If you're recording the wishes on
tape, have each person give his or her name
before completing the sentence.

29 Capsule IV: Lesson Sounds

Tape-record your Sunday school lesson. Give the
date and introduce your class by each person
(students and teachers) saying his or her name.
Then tape a reading of the Bible story, class
discussion, memory passage recitation, and any
other parts you wish.

30 Up with the Sun!

Have your children ever seen the sun rise? Invite kids for a "sleepover" and plan to get up early before the sun is up. Pack some cocoa, and drive to a good vantage point (park, forest preserve, lakeside). Help kids think about the sun through these activities: Ask how many times a year the sun rises. Challenge kids to figure out how many times it has risen since they were born. During your sunrise quiet time together, thank God for His faithfulness.

31 Hey, Take a Walk

What's fall like in your part of the country? Sunny and warm? Cold and windy? In most places, fall is a time of outdoor changes—a great time to hike around and see what's happening.

Plan a walk. A city park or forest preserve, a country road, or even a vacant lot will do.

Collect your gear. Ask different kids to bring such items as a sharp knife or pruning shears, a knapsack for collecting things, a magnifying glass and field glasses, several baby food jars with holes punched in the lids, and a snack.

Now, Go! Open your eyes to the beauty of God's creation. Be as quiet as possible—you want to observe nature, not interrupt it. Keep all your senses alert.

LISTEN . . . for bird songs, the wind in dry grass and fallen leaves, the scurrying of wildlife. Sit still for a few minutes and just listen.

SMELL . . . a distant bonfire, the crisp air, the freshness of pine needles, smoke from chimneys.

TOUCH . . . the roughness of cones, bark, lichen; the softness of dried grass, moss, a feather; the smoothness of weathered wood.

LOOK . . . closely at the beauty around you. What are the colors of fall? How is nature getting itself ready for winter? Look for animal tracks. Study them carefully. Can you identify the creature that made them?

Finish the day by reading Psalm 104. Did the nature walk help kids understand the feelings of that psalm writer? How about writing your own psalm together about God's wonderful world?

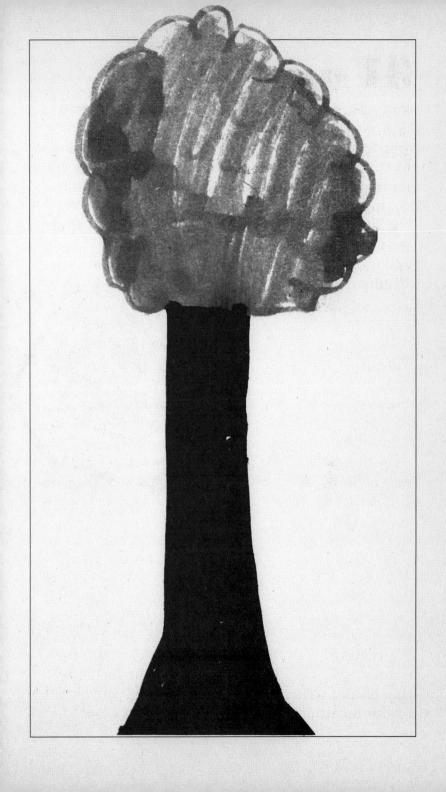

32 The Name Game

Play the Name Game to thank God for the wonderful things He created. As you walk through a wooded area, tell children to look for something to thank God for that starts with the same letter as their name. For example, Sally might say, "I thank God for the sun." Then Randy might say, "Sally thanks God for the sun, and I thank God for rain." See how many times you can go around the group without forgetting anyone's "thank-You."

33 Creation Party

Have a creation party at a nearby park or back-yard. After reading Genesis 1, play a game for each day of Creation. Here are some game suggestions.

Day 1—God created light. *Game:* Take a light-less hike. Blindfold everyone but the leader. Hike single file, with each person touching the shoulders of the one in front of him or her.

Day 2—God made the sky. *Games:* (1) Try to keep a ball in the air as you toss it around. (2) Have a paper airplane contest.

Day 3—God separated water and land. *Games:* (1) Toss around a water balloon. (2) Have a soap bubble contest.

Day 4—God made sun, moon, and stars. *Game:* Play shadow tag (don't let *It* step on your shadow or you are *It*).

Day 5—God made fish and birds. *Game:* Un-scramble the mixed-up names of fish and birds (e.g., nribo = robin).

Day 6—God made people. *Game:* Get in a circle. Tell what you really like about the person on your right and on your left. You'll all feel great when you've finished.

Day 7—God rested. Serve refreshments and pray thank-You prayers for God's creation.

34 Snow Fun

• Paint a snow message. Put water and food coloring in a squeeze bottle. Paint your message on fresh snow.
• Look for animal tracks after a snowfall—how many can you identify?
• Instead of just a snowman, how about making a snow family? Or snow animals?

35 Feathery Finds

Ask children to be on the lookout for feathers. Birds molt regularly, and you can collect feathers of many shapes and colors. When you have a good variety, tie them with different lengths of thread on a coat hanger or dowel rod for a feather mobile. Try to name each feather by using a book like *Peterson's Field Guide to the Birds of North America.*

36 Buggy Browsing

Under rocks and logs, on branches, in the dirt—
challenge kids to see how many kinds of bugs
they can catch. Make a bug keeper by putting
some moist grass and leaves in a large, wide-
mouthed glass jar. To give the bugs air, punch
holes in the lid, or cover the opening with
cheesecloth or a piece of nylon stocking. Help
kids find the names of their bugs in an insect
guide like the *Audubon Society Field Guide to
North American Insects and Spiders*. Be sure to
let the bugs go after an hour or two.

37 Seed Search

It's not hard to find seeds; some of them will find
you! As you hike in the woods, thistle seeds will
stick to your socks and winged maple seeds may
get tangled in your hair. To see what you've
found, bring along a book like *Weeds*, by D. C.
Hogner. Show off your seed collection in the
bottom half of an egg carton by taping a seed in
each cup.

MISSIONS ACTIVITIES

38 A Looong Letter

Buy a roll of adding machine paper. Begin writing a long, skinny letter to one of your church missionaries. Pass the roll to other kids and adults so they can add to the letter. When the roll is filled, send it to the missionary. This is a fun way to encourage God's workers. You are letting those who work for Him in a foreign country know that you are remembering and praying for them. (Check with the post office to make sure your missionary will not have to pay a tax to get the rolled-up letter.)

39 Mission Fund Raiser

Raise money for a special missionary project by putting on a garage sale. Work with parents or several families together to collect things they no longer use. Make posters and flyers to advertise the garage sale. Display another poster at the garage sale that explains where the money raised will be used. When people come, be ready to tell them about the missionary project.

40 At-Home Missionaries

Find out what it is like to be a missionary who teaches the Bible to people who have never read God's Word. Plan to teach a Bible verse or story to some little kids. Think of a fun way to help them understand it—a puppet show, a skit, a song, or drawing. Invite younger brothers and sisters and neighbors about three to six years old. These children can't read the Bible yet, so—like the people many missionaries teach—they will count on you to teach them the truth about Jesus.

41 Care Package

Find out from your pastor or the missions chairperson of your church what items you can begin to save to send to medical missionaries. Some things might be: empty pill bottles, bandages torn from sheets, cotton balls. Once you have a list, print up several copies and pass them around to church families and neighbors so they can help, too. On the bottom of each list you hand out, print the verse from Luke: 4:40. Pray for the missionaries who carry on the healing work of Jesus.

42 Prayer Power

Use "prayer power" to help Christians who are working in churches all over the world. Keep a world map or globe in a prominent place. With push pins or stars, mark where you live. Then mark the countries on the map where the missionaries live and work that your church supports. If possible, tape their pictures on the map. Each week choose one country and pray for the pastors, missionaries, and church workers there who are helping people learn about God. The next week, choose a new country to pray for.

See what an atlas or encyclopedia says about the weather, customs, language, land, and history of the country you choose. Imagine what churches in this country might be like. How would they be different from your church?

43 Overseas Pen Pal

If you know a missionary family overseas, write and ask if they can locate a pen pal for your children—a missionary child or national child about the same age. As a class you might make a cassette tape recording to send to this new friend in addition to letters. Include brief interviews of class members, group singing, and favorite Bible verses.

44 Adopt a Child

A number of mission agencies have adopt-a-child programs. This is an excellent way for children to be personally involved in mission work. If your children receive an allowance, they could give a tithe to help support a needy child. (You will probably have to make up the difference—total cost is usually $10 to $15 per month.) You can write letters to the child, pray for him or her, and usually receive letters in return.

45 International Guests

Make a deliberate attempt to invite as guests international students, recent immigrants, former missionaries, or missionaries home on furlough. Ask lots of questions. Get them to tell stories. Have them teach the children a few words or phrases in their native (or adopted) language.

46 'When I Grow Up . . .'

See how many occupations kids can think of in three minutes that would be helpful on the mission field. When you talk with children about what they want to be when they grow up, instill the idea that they could do many different things as missionaries. Missionaries are teachers and airplane pilots and farmers and construction workers and writers and doctors and pastors— just like the Christian people who do these things in our own country.

47 A Huge Task

Do some research to determine what percent of the people of a certain country is Christian. To provide a visual reminder for kids of the need for people in that country to hear the Good News, obtain two large glass jars. Label one jar "Christians" and the other "Non-Christians." Fill the jars with objects such as kernels of corn, pennies, or marbles according to the percentage that that country is Christian. For example, if 12% of that country is Christian, put 12 items in that jar and 88 items in the jar marked Non-Christian. Clearly identify the country you've researched so that children will realize how greatly the Gospel is needed in that country.

CHURCH ACTIVITIES

48 Mini-Tour Guides

Help visitors at church feel right at home by
having kids offer to be mini-tour guides. Organize kids to shake hands and introduce themselves. Show visitors around the church: the
coat racks, location of rest rooms, the class-
rooms. Introduce their new friends to others
they pass during the mini-tour. You'll want to
make name tags for the tour guides.

49 Pastor Praise

• Make a "We Like Pastor" poster. Print the pastor's name on the picture. Have kids sign their
names and write notes of appreciation. Or copy
the following Bible verses: Romans 10:17; Isaiah
52:7; Colossians 1:28; Timothy 3:1. Secretly
tape the poster to the pastor's study door.
• Leave an occasional plate of cookies or fruit on
your pastor's desk. Tie it nicely with plastic wrap
and a bow. Attach a card that says "With love
from your friends," and sign your names.
• Find out when your pastor's birthday is. Then
remind everyone to send a card in order to get a
whole mailbox full. Kids might want to chip in
and buy a nice flowering plant for the pastor's
office.

50 Nice and Neat

Make hall and room neatness reminders for your church building. Cut large arrows out of construction or poster paper. Glue a wad of crumpled paper to each arrow and tape the arrows—the tips pointing down—on walls above waste containers. Next to the arrows, tape another strip of poster board with neatly lettered words of Psalm 26:8 or Psalm 122:1.

51 Able Helpers

Talk to church leaders about letting kids from your class help adult workers during one service. Those who work with greeters can hold the door and shake hands; musicians' helpers might turn pages; those who work with ushers can help pass out bulletins and show visitors to their seats.

52 Secret Worship

Plan an underground Christian meeting. Pretend you live in a country where you are not allowed to worship openly or own a Bible. So you meet in secret. Light the room with one candle. Talk softly. Share all the Bible verses you have memorized. Pray for Christians who really have to meet like this.

53 Treat the Leader

Let kids choose one (or two or three) church leaders to invite out for ice cream or a soft drink. Have kids chip in their own money to pay for the treat themselves. Or choose someone they'd like to get to know better. Tell that person how much you appreciate his or her work in the church and that you are praying for him or her.

54 Book Party

Plan a book party. Have each kid bring a favorite book to give to the church library. Paste a note in the front of the book explaining just a little of what the book is about. Read Philippians 4:8 together and talk about why it's important to read Christian books.

55 Worship Helpers

If your church has a separate worship service for little children, the help of older school kids might be welcome there. Help kids plan things they might do: play the piano, read Scripture, help little ones memorize verses, or even teach a Bible story using puppets or flannelgraph figures.

HELPING ACTIVITIES

56 Adopt a Grandparent

Many older people have a hard time getting out to church in cold weather. How about considering having the class adopt an older member of your congregation? Plan to visit that person each week. Here are some things you could do:
• Bring your church bulletin and talk about new things and events in the church.
• Share stories from your Sunday school lesson.
• Sing a song together.
• Read a psalm with that person each week. (Psalms 23, 63, 98, 100, 117, 121 are good ones.)

57 Three-Star Work Week

Have children make a list of home chores their parents don't enjoy doing. Tell them to put stars beside the things they could help with. Challenge them to do at least three stars' worth of work for their moms or dads this week.

58 Fun Helpers

Encourage kids to plan a special summer activity for little children in their neighborhood. The kids should pick something the little ones would enjoy and help them plan it. Let the little kids be in charge; the big kids should work behind the scenes to make sure everything goes right. *Some ideas:* a treasure hunt; a pet show; a kiddie circus. What other ideas do the kids have? Tell them to remember that their job is to help the little ones have fun!

Read Mark 10:35-45. See how unlike James and John the helpers can be.

59 Welcome Team

Organize a "Welcome Team" to serve Jesus and to help a new family in your area. Moving can be discouraging. Parents have a lot of work to do. Boys and girls may be lonely and need to make new friends. The family will have to learn their way around the new neighborhood.

You could take the new family on a tour of the neighborhood, then invite them for dessert. Tell about your schools and stores. Play a game together. Invite them to go to church and Sunday school with you. Tell what you like about your church and why it is important to you.

60 Study Pals

Does your child have a classmate who does not speak English very well because he or she was born in another country? Encourage your child to offer to help this person after school with homework. After the study session, play a game together. Maybe the new friend can teach a new game! A group of children could all pitch in to buy this new person an easy-to-read Christian book or Bible.

61 The Mop Mob

Tackle a summer work project for your church. Look around the church to see what needs fixing or cleaning. Talk with your pastor about project ideas. Then issue a call for help among other families or Sunday school classes. Meet with volunteers to plan when and how you will do the work. Pray that God will help you. Then get busy!

62 Pet Service

Are your children great animal lovers? Then a good summer project may be pet-sitting. Encourage them to contact people who are going on vacation and offer to take care of their pets. Children could also include newspaper and mail service. If the children bring the pets home with them, be sure they clear it with the whole family.

63 Yard Service

Suggest to your kids that they organize a yard-service project. If they get paid for their work, the money could go to a mission project or a need within your church. Some advice to pass on to your child:
• Set up a regular day to work on a lawn.
• Be prompt and dependable and hard-working.
• Learn the difference between the flowers and the weeds.
• Always accept treats of cold drinks or ice cream with a smile and a "Thank you."
    Kids may love to think up their own service project ideas.

64 Refreshment Stand

Your kids may make mountains of cookies or squeeze luscious lemonade, but if they live on a back street, they'll never get people to buy their goodies. Solution? Go where the crowds are— garage sales, block parties, play lots, etc. Locate a choice spot and ask permission to set up there. *Advice for kids:* Make your cookies BIG, have your drinks icy cold, and be clean!

65 Need in the News

Look through the newspaper to find an article about someone who is in trouble and needs help. The Bible tells us that God will help those who call on Him. Maybe the person in the story doesn't know God wants to help. Describe the situation to your children and encourage them to pray that God will help this person trust Him. Find out the person's address and have the kids write a letter to him or her. Here are some verses to share: Psalms 18:3; 55:16, 17; 46:1; 86:5-7; 145:18, 19. Try to find out how God answers their prayers.

66 Bike Wash

Youth groups often hold car washes. Why not have your kids hold a bike wash? Encourage people in your church neighborhood to bring their bicycles, tricycles, Big Wheels, and skateboards. Supply a hose, buckets, soaps, rags, and towels. This could be a fundraiser or a service for your church neighborhood just out of love.

67 Help in Trouble

Do the children know someone who is facing a tough problem right now? Encourage them to do something special to help the person in trouble.

Ideas: Promise to pray for him each day; give her a compliment to encourage her; copy the words of Isaiah 41:10 on a nice card and leave this secret message from God where the person will find it. Or several children could work to together to make a giant-size card out of poster board.

INDIVIDUAL ACTIVITIES

68 Far-Out Forgiveness

If kids have bad feelings toward someone, challenge them to try one of these far-out ways to forgive:

• Send a mystery invitation to meet for a treat. Don't sign your name. Do show up and say you'd like to be friends again.

• Write your apology in a letter, cut it up like a jigsaw puzzle, and send it.

• Make up clues for a treasure hunt; hide the first one in your friend's desk at school. You can be waiting with a snack treasure (cookies, a candy bar) that the two of you can share.

69 An All-Day Pray

No, this doesn't mean kids should spend the whole day on their knees. It does mean thinking of God, thanking Him, or asking His help in everything they do. It does mean listening in quiet moments for Him to speak to them. After the all-day pray, have them choose some special times they'd like to keep on praying regularly—when they first wake up, right after lunch, etc. The all-day pray will help them discover times that work well.

70 Prayer Log

Encourage kids to keep a log of their prayer requests. In this notebook they could copy verses about trusting God and His timing at the bottom each page. Start with these: Psalm 46:10; James 1:3, 4; Romans 8:28; I Peter 5:7. They should leave room to record how and when God answered their prayers. Keeping track of God's answers will build up their faith in Him.

71 Prayer Check

Have kids run a prayer check on themselves. They should start by listing some good prayer habits.

☐ I pray for others.
☐ I truly believe God hears me.
☐ I will accept whatever answer God sends.
☐ I thank God often.
☐ I look for God's answers.

Have them grade themselves on each prayer habit. They can tuck this list in their Bibles for a month; then check to see how their prayer habits are improving.

72 T.L.I.M.L.*

Mystery messages are a fun way to witness for God at school. Have kids make up mystery messages using the first letters of words from verses that mean something to them. Guess these mystery messages?

• F.G.S.L.T.W. (See John 3:16.)
• R.I.T.L.A. (See Philippians 4:4.)

They can write their own mystery message from God's Word on their notebooks or on letters they send to friends. Sooner or later, someone will ask them to explain the message. Their explanation will tell that person something important about God. When one mystery is solved, they can switch to a new message.

(*Check Psalm 27:1.)

73 My Spiritual Diary

Challenge kids to start spiritual diaries. They can use spiral notebooks to make daily entries about how God helped them that day. Did He give calmness during a hard test? Did they pray for courage to resist a temptation? Were they able to talk to Him when they felt hurt by a friend? With each entry, they should thank the Lord for helping them. They can read their notebooks when their faith needs a boost. Seeing how God has helped in the past will give more faith for the future.

74 Congratulations!

Have kids spread happiness around with congratulation notes. When someone at school does well on a test or wins a prize or finishes a difficult task, they can send a note to let him or her know they're glad about it. They could draw a cartoon or a big smiley face and a note saying, "Congratulations—you deserve it!" or, "You're the greatest!"

75 Personal Time Capsule

Imagine what God might want your kids to be doing in the year 2010. Have them write a prediction about how each of these Bible verses will apply to them in the future: Genesis 2:24; Proverbs 1:5, I Timothy 6:17; Matthew 28:19, 20. Then they can make a time capsule by sealing their predictions in a container and keeping it unopened in their dresser drawers until 2010. Then they'll see how God works out His plan for them.

76 TV Tests

• Have children be lie detectors as they watch TV commercials. Are the commercials obeying God's commandment to tell the truth about their products? Parents can help them write letters about untruthful commercials.

• Ask them to make lists of the Ten Commandments from Exodus 20:3-17. Instruct them to place their lists and pencils close to the TV. As they watch TV, they should notice every time one of the Ten Commandments is broken and make a mark by that commandment. Which commandment gets broken most often on TV?

• Have them determine how they think God would rate the TV programs they watch? Would God most likely be pleased or angered or sad by what is shown on a program. They can rate the show by giving it a number from 1 to 10 (1 is the worst and 10 is the best).

77 A Gift of Time

Challenge kids to give a gift of time by playing with a neighbor's preschool child so the mother can have some time off. Don't accept money. Explain that this is their gift of time to Jesus. Preschoolers love to be read to. Kids could keep a list of the books they read to these little tykes.

78 A Real Hero

Read about the kind of heroes God wants—see Matthew 5;10, 43, 44; 18:4; 20:26. Have the kids use their names in an acrostic. They can write the letters of their names down the side of a piece of paper; then write a word beginning with each letter telling the kind of hero they'd like to be. They can tape this on their mirrors and pray that God will help them be this way.

79 Promise Chain

Kids can make a promise chain using Bible verses that tell about God's promise of forgiveness. Each time they find a forgiveness verse, they can write it on a strip of paper and link it to the chain. Here are some verses to get them started: Colossians 3:13; I John 1:9; Matthew 6;14; Psalm 103:3.

80 Lunch Buddy

Ask children to share their lunchtime with someone who may be lonely. Next time they enter the school cafeteria, suggest that they don't head for their usual group of friends. They should look for someone who's alone and join him or her and make a new friend!

81 Dessert x 2

Suggest that in their school lunches, kids pack an extra dessert for someone they don't get along with. While they eat together they could say that they'd like to be friends. Then they should pray for that person and watch God's love get results!

82 Double It

Double your pleasure and fun—not with chewing gum but with money given to God. Challenge kids to tell God that they will give Him the same amount of money they spend on themselves this week. If they buy a pack of gum, they should set aside the same amount to give to God through your church. They'll have to do without some treats, but they can ask God to double their pleasure in giving.

83 My Own Tabernacle

Discuss with the kids the benefits of have a special place to be alone with God. Here are a couple of suggestions you could give them:
• Create your own "tabernacle"—a quiet place where you can go to worship God. This could be in your room, a tree house, or a tent you make from a blanket. Go to your tabernacle every day.
• Did you ever pray or read your Bible in a tree, in the middle of a wheat field, in your closet, under a table? Try moving your Bible study time to as many unique, quiet places as you can think of. Let these new settings help you pray new prayers as you make new discoveries.

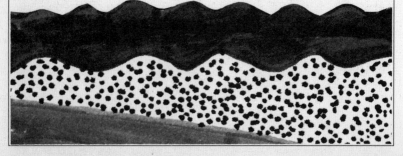

84 Super Sermon

Suggest that children try these ideas to help them get more out of the sermon in your church's worship service.

1. *Take notes.* Try to write the main ideas so you can use your notes to tell people what the sermon was about.

2. As the pastor preaches, *write one thing you will do this week* to follow what the sermon teaches.

3. After the service, *tell the pastor* what you enjoyed most about the sermon.

4. *Ask other people* what they liked most about the sermon.

5. Wait until Saturday and *write what you remember* about last Sunday's sermon.

85 Surprise Day

Encourage children to plan a "Surprise Day" for their families. They can think of something nice they could do for each person in the family. They shouldn't let the family know that they're the helpers. They could leave notes saying, "Surprise! See I Corinthians 3:9." After they have done all their surprises, they could tell their families that they were helping God by helping them. Read the surprise verse again and discuss ways different family members can help God by helping each other.

FAMILY ACTIVITIES

Here are some ideas you can use with your own family, or photocopy them and send them home for the kids in your class to use with their families.

86 Yummy Treats

• Spread slices of apple, peach, and banana on a cookie sheet. Leave in a sunny window or let sit in a slightly warm oven until dried. They're better than potato chips!
• Mix together a few handfuls of uncooked oatmeal, wheat germ, chopped nuts, raisins, coconut, and honey. Spread on a greased cookie sheet and bake overnight at 200°.

87 Alphabet Thank-You

To begin, one person names something he or she is thankful for which begins with the letter A. The next person repeats this and adds something he or she is thankful for which begins with the letter B. Take turns having each person try to remember the entire list beginning with A and adding something for the next letter.

88 I-Like-My-Family Night!

Plan a special night to enjoy each other as a family. Here are some ideas; add your own to these!

• Each person should give everyone else in the family a word gift. Say something nice about each person.

• Make happy-face cookies together. Have each person decorate a flat cookie with a happy face to give to the person next oldest in age (the oldest would give to the youngest). If you have cookies left over, share them with people you know would enjoy a smile.

• Read Bible verses about family happiness. Put them together in a poem—Romans 12:10; 5:2; Proverbs 16:20; Isaiah 12:2-5.

89 Family Rules

Start a notebook of family rules. Take some of them right from the Bible and make up others of your own. Look up Matthew 22:37-39; 5:44; Exodus 20:12; and Ephesians 5:2. Get together to discuss the rules you choose and plan how you'll enforce them. Review your rules at a family council once a month.

90 'Best Things' Game

Play a "Best Things" game at dinner. Tell a best thing that happened this year. Then someone else tells a best thing. After sharing, join hands and thank God for His gifts.

Here are some variations on this mealtime discussion activity: most embarrassing moment in the past year; the funniest thing that happened; answers to prayer; the time you were most frightened; the thing you're most thankful for; something that seemed bad but turned out to be good.

91 Family Servants

Read John 13:14-16 together as a family to see how Jesus served His disciples. Have a family ceremony where each serves the others. *Ideas:* wash feet, give back rubs, serve snack, shine shoes.

92 God Takes Care of Us

Get your family together for a special time of praise for how God takes care of you. Think of different family emergencies that turned out all right (*example:* car trouble on vacation). Act them out for other family members to guess. Praise God for His protection and care in those situations.

Memorize Psalm 121:2 together. Encourage children to say this verse to themselves every time they come to a "Red Sea crisis"—a big problem or scary situation of their own. It will remind them that God is there to help.

93 Family Coat of Arms

Long ago each family had a coat of arms, a sign that told what was special about the family. Have your family draw a coat of arms, a shield or crest, to tell what is special about you. Would any of these Bible verses make a good motto for your coat of arms? See Isaiah 12:2, Psalm 9:1, and Psalm 27:1.

94 Prayer for Justice

Start an exciting new prayer list. Give family members a stack of this week's newspapers and magazines. Scan them for stories of people who are being treated unfairly in your community or in the world. (You should have no trouble finding these.) When everyone has read the paper, clip out the stories you chose. Stick them up on a wall or your refrigerator. Pray for these people after each evening meal. Try to keep tabs on what happens to them. Think of ways (letters, phone calls) that your family might help fight this injustice.

95 Dinner Guest

Add a "Jesus chair" to your family dinner table. When children set the table, tell them to make a place for one guest—chair and dishes. Reassure your family that you can count, and explain that the extra chair is a reminder that Jesus is with you all the time—even when you eat. How do you react with a "Jesus chair" at the table? Is your conversation the same? How about your manners?

96 Future Fun

Have some "future fun" with your family. Pretend you're stepping into a time machine headed into the future. "Stop" the machine after five years, ten years, 25 years. Look at yourselves in those periods of your lives. What do you each look like? What are you each doing? How will your faith in Jesus help you face what lies ahead?

97 Hunger Jar

Let kids decorate a jar, using tempera paints or gluing on macaroni or rick rack in designs. Label the jar, "Hunger Jar." At the end of each day, have everyone in the family search pockets and purses for pennies. Deposit these in the jar. When the jar is full, donate the money to a group that supplies food for hungry people.

98 Giver Reward

Create a traveling "Giver Award" for your family. It should be something to wear—a cap or a button. The first one to be a *giver* can wear the award until he or she can pass it on to another *giver*. Giving might mean sharing the last piece of pizza, giving a backrub, letting someone else choose the TV show, or helping with the dishes.

99 Postcard Plaudits

In Romans 16:1-16 Paul mentioned some church members who had worked very hard for the Lord. Are there some people in your church that your family admires for their courage and hard work? Send them a postcard telling how you feel. You'll be an encourager.

100 Family Tradition Notebook

Together with other family members, make a list of every family tradition you can think of—special things that your family does the same way every time. Here are some things to consider:

- Christmas
- Birthdays
- Easter
- Vacations
- Meal times
- Other holidays

Fill the pages of this notebook with photographs, drawings, and journal entries about these traditions.

Then spend some time discussing new traditions that you and your family would like to begin during this next year.